MODERN DIVORCE
AND MEDIATION

MODERN DIVORCE AND MEDIATION

Dr. Roham Ghassemi

To order additional copies of this book, contact:
Xlibris
844-714-8691
www.Xlibris.com
Orders@Xlibris.com
849999

To my teacher and guide, Professor Nader Angha, who has always encouraged all his students to educate themselves in different fields and on all levels and who suggested to me to enter the field of mediation.

Roham Ghassemi has been a Mediator since 2004 and has been mediating both civil and family mediation for nonprofit organizations, such as DMS, Dallas County Dispute Resolution Services, and Southern Methodist University as a volunteer mediator. He is a full-time mediator for TDI Texas Department of Insurance and operates a private mediation service. He also holds a BS in Business CCU, MS in Psychology CCU, MLA in Negotiation SMU as well as a PhD in Psychology from CCU. He is a certified Mediator and a Certified Divorce Mediator. He has a corporate sector negotiation Certificate along with his real estate license in Texas Since 1996.

Author of books:
Substance Abuse and Cognitive behavioral therapy
Motivation and Knowledge

CONTENTS

Introduction

The purpose of this book is to provide a brief explanation of mediation, specifically divorce mediation. It talks about the many benefits of divorce mediation over the adversarial process, which involves two attorneys representing the two sides to negotiate and argue on their behalf.

"In mediation you remain in control of the process, instead of taking the risk of fighting in a courtroom where a judge may make the decisions neither of you wants" (Carol A. Butler and Dolores D. Walker, *Divorce Mediation Answer Book*, [1999], 3).

The reason I have called this book *Modern Divorce* is because of the way everything around us is taking a new modern path in our everyday lives, especially after the pandemic. We were forced to learn new ways to communicate and new ways to balance work, life, and family, and new ways to get to our goals. Even by having conflicts and disputes, it is much more efficient to get results through telecommunication or video conferences than through the in-person model.

"The pandemic changed our lives at work and home. Video and audio conferences replaced most face to face meetings including mediation. Now there is much anticipation and hope that face to face meetings will begin again since more of the population is being vaccinated. However, it is unlikely that all mediations will revert back to the pre-pandemic mode" (Thomas Repicky, Cleveland Metropolitan Bar Association, July 20, 2021).

This is no exception in getting a divorce. As more and more people realize the practical way to go through a divorce, they understand the benefits of going to mediation sessions. As divorce can be a highly stressful circumstance, it is important to reduce the stress level as much as possible by going to a mediator in a comfortable environment, which can be in the comfort of your own home. From the way we communicate with one another to the way we research everything, we are interested in ways of doing everything simpler, more effective, and more convenient.

In most settings we can see individuals develop new skills and experiences during the pandemic. Whole population has been forced into a crash course on modern technology, and the benefitual result is more people than ever have skills and knowledge to work effectively and get more work done from anywhere.

As everyone is preoccupied with living their everyday life, society has developed in a significantly more modern way. As time goes by, more and more people are getting familiar with mediation. They have experienced and learned the importance of mediation as it reflects on the way they do things and resolve conflicts. Mediation has shown and is continuing to show how it helps resolve issues and conflicts in the workplace and even in families. Most people have had some experience with mediation, for example, when siblings have an argument and the parents intervene. The parent acts as the mediator, or when students in a classroom have a conflict and the teacher intervenes; the teacher acts as the mediator.

Growth creates opportunity, and with it comes the need to adjust which can lead to conflict. Mediation is one of the most successful tools for dealing with conflict and is an addition to the legal system. In the last few years, mediation has found its way into almost every contract that we sign.

For example in real estate contracts, "Mediation: it is the policy of state of Texas to encourage resolution of disputes throCugh alternative dispute resolution procedures such as mediation" (Texas Real Estate Commission (TREC), "One to Four Family Contract," p. 7, par. 16).

"We agree to go to mediation when a dispute rises before taking matters further," which has changed lives and the way we do business. At the same time, mediation has saved people from a lot of stress, headache, time, and money when people do have a dispute.

Knowing how everything is changing around us, we are learning to change our behavior as well. To be able to benefit from what this alternative has to offer, we have learned to be more practical and rational in comparison to being frustrated and emotional. We use the help of these new tools and information to find answers and get past all the things that keep us from gaining full control over our lives when issues come up.

Getting a divorce may top the chart in conflicts, not only do you have to dissolve your marriage contract, but you also have to separate yourself from an environment and relationship, in which you were accustomed to living for a long time, that's becoming baneful. The relationship that you entered with certain beliefs, understandings, and judgments, you must now learn how to live without and change your ways. That's why so many of your feelings and emotions are involved when getting a divorce. Since it is not as simple as just talking about putting feelings aside and just focusing on dissolving the marriage contract, the process may become very complicated and uncomfortable, especially if you don't have the basic expectation of what you are going to face and be prepared for.

When there is a conflict with a contract, it is obvious we can hire an attorney to have a better understanding of the contract and our options to negotiate are based on what is written, but in circumstances like a divorce, your emotions are involved. You can't just always go and dissolve a relationship as you do in a simple contract. There are so many other aspects to consider to ensure closure is received as it's not like a simple resignation from a job where you can put in a two-week notice and it's done.

In a regular contract, feelings and emotions are not that involved, and therefore, you are not under so much stress about your life and your children's lives. Since the future life and finances for you and your children are to be affected by this decision, lots of unanswered questions come to mind. These questions and all the unknowns and lack of control/knowledge in divorce are the main reasons we feel vulnerable. It makes us just want someone to take over and solve our problems, but with less understanding of the process comes less control of the outcome and of closure. Not only is it not helpful, but it will also prolong the process and the cost involved to have an attorney do it on your behalf. Mediation in most divorce cases is beneficial when you understand the divorce process and can make your own decisions and get the results quickly. The main reason why mediation is a beneficial option provided is so you can get a chance to have your voice and your own ideas heard and to be part of the process along with having more control of the outcome.

"Probably 80 percent of divorcing couples are better off mediating, the others should let their lawyers negotiate for them. Although most couples can work out fair and reasonable agreement with the help of a mediator, some are stymied for a variety of reasons" (Paula James, *The Divorce Mediation Handbook* [1997], 17).

To have control of the outcome is the most important matter in every dispute. It is important to have the option to express your feelings and see if they are being heard so that you may be able to get some closure and satisfaction. Besides the agony and stress, can you imagine the time and money that you must spend on all these communications? Rather than getting to your goal to get through your divorce as soon as possible through mediation, in an adversarial divorce, time is not of the essence for the attorneys representing you. Instead of turning your marriage contract to an attorney and letting him or her communicate on your behalf with another attorney who is speaking on behalf of your spouse (which prolongs weekly issues through a series of back-and-forth communication), the option of going to mediation speeds up the process. The sooner you can end the period you go through a divorce, the sooner you can start your new life and start over again.

The way we communicate with our society today gives us more information, so we can do more things our way. When we are interested to be involved in the outcome of something as important as our divorce, mediation gives us the chance to be more engaged in the whole process and outcome. This is what I call modern divorce.

"Advocate of divorce mediation research has focused on outcomes such as settlement rates, cost efficiency, client satisfaction, effect on levels of conflict and cooperation, psychological adjustment, and compliance. Despite methodological problems limiting generalizations, most studies report mildly favorable to very positive findings. Research on the mediation process and mediator behaviors has received very limited attention, and should be the focus of the next decade of research to elevate the mediation field to a more sophisticated, effective level of practice" (Joan B. Kelly, March 15, 2005).

When you go through mediation, you are trying to resolve your conflict in the most sufficient and modern way. And you are involved in every step and every term of separation. In many cases today, there is no need for the traditional path that is still being used to have two lawyers negotiate and find solutions on your behalf by following a set of outlines by the court and the judge and so limit your decision-making.

With getting a divorce, one has to sue the other spouse to get the divorce process started for your marriage to be dissolved. They start with a lawsuit, and they continue until they can get the most out of the lawsuit; that includes assets, property, and the children.

"Divorce requires a Lawsuit. One of you must sue the other in order to dissolve your marriage. In doing so, you automatically become adversaries. The law says so" (James, *Divorce Mediation Handbook*, 3).

In the business world, it is much easier to dissolve an association, whether it is a company or a partnership, when there is conflict and they are not willing to use mediation. Lawyers can put everything in black and white and negotiate without considering all the emotions and feelings involved in dissolving the relationship. But in a marriage, there are so much more personalities involved; emotions and feelings are under stress and most vulnerable, and those are what make the separation complicated. That is the reason it requires both sides' direct decisions and acceptance involved simultaneously and directly, especially when there are children involved besides the number of assets or debt. The relationship between parents never ends. As partners, you may dissolve your marriage, but you will always be a mom and a dad in your children's lives. So it is much more beneficial, especially when there are children involved, to have this conflict resolved without leaving deep scars on one another and also learn to have the best possible relationship as parents in the future.

Divorce with children is probably the most important issue in divorce. That is one of the main reasons people don't think about divorce to begin with. They worry about their feelings and emotions, they worry about the scars on the children, and they worry about how they feel in the future about what mom and dad decided to do so many years back. With mediation, a lot of those concerns are being mentioned and even helped to find answers. They are also allowed to be mentioned easier and to get to a solution that works for everyone, in comparison to talking about subjects concerning children to get to an answer and having to revisit the same issue again in a few days. In the modern world, we like and prefer to make our decisions right then and not postpone it to a later time; therefore, we just can't make decisions while not knowing when to have the outcome and result back. We make decisions based on the outcome. Having an adversarial divorce, it is like disputing without having options to know the results right there, like the concerns about the arrangements after the divorce and not knowing the other party's reaction and thinking about one's options.

For most couples who prefer a quicker result for dissolving their marriage, mediation may be the best way to close this chapter of their life and help have a better beginning of the next chapter of life with the feeling that they have gotten closure on the important issues that have importance to them and their family. Now you are ready to start the next chapter.

CHAPTER 1

What is mediation and divorce mediation

Mediation is a confidential conference where all the participants attend to cooperate to resolve the dispute between them. All negotiations during mediation are nonbinding and confidential. Experience has shown that mediation is more effective because it is confidential.

"Mediation is a form of dispute resolution that allows individuals and/or organizations involved in a dispute to work together toward resolving their own differences. During mediation, trained mediators work closely with the disputing parties by listening to all sides of the dispute, identifying areas of concern, and exploring underlying interests and possible solutions. The mediation process gives parties the opportunity to tell their story and to hear the other person while focusing on moving forward. Mediators remain neutral throughout the process and unlike a magistrate or judge, mediators do not decide the outcome; the outcome is determined by the parties themselves" (Harvard Mediation Program, "What Mediation Is," https://clinics. law.harvard.edu/hmp/what-mediation-is/).

The parties must be present in person at mediation. Where a party is not a natural person (for example a company), a properly authorized person with written authority to settle the matter is required to represent it.

If each party is prepared to negotiate in good faith and work toward a mutually satisfying compromise, the mediation is more likely to succeed. Parties who are not prepared to make concessions will be better served by the traditional adversarial system of the court process.

> The mediator helps each person evaluate their needs and goals for reaching a solution. All decisions are made by the parties, not the mediator. A mediator may be selected by the parties based upon a recommendation by a friend, attorney, therapist, or another professional. Mediators are also listed in the yellow pages. The courts will often provide a list of mediators. In some situations, a list of approved mediators is provided to select from.
>
> Most mediators receive formal classroom-style training. Some participate in apprenticeships or in mentoring programs. While training alone does not guarantee a competent mediator, most professional mediators have had some type of formal training. Important considerations in selecting a mediator include, among others, fee structure, his or her number of years of mediation, the number of mediations conducted, and types of mediations conducted." (USLegalForms.com, "What Is Mediation," www. uslegalforms.com/mediation/)

One of the underlying philosophies in mediation is that the parties can reach a settlement that does not necessarily conform to legal precedent or to community standards but is one which resolves the problem to the satisfaction of the parties.

Therefore, any settlement reached as a result of the mediation session is written down by the parties and signed by each side. The terms of the settlement may be retained in contract form, or if there are court proceedings, the lawyers will obtain the appropriate court order.

Mediation, as used in law, is a form of alternative dispute resolution (ADR), a way of resolving disputes between two or more parties with concrete effects. Typically, a third party, the mediator, assists the parties to negotiate a settlement. Disputants may mediate disputes in a variety of domains, such as commercial, legal, diplomatic, workplace, community, and family matters.

"The term 'mediation' broadly refers to any instance in which a third party helps others reach agreement. More specifically, mediation has a structure, timetable and dynamics that 'ordinary' negotiation lacks. The process is private and confidential, possibly enforced by law. Participation is typically voluntary. The mediator acts as a neutral third party and facilitates rather than directs the process. Mediators use various techniques to open, or improve, dialogue between disputants, aiming to help the parties reach an agreement. Much depends on the mediator's skill and training. As the practice gained popularity, training programs, certifications and licensing followed, producing trained professional mediators committed to the discipline" (*Wikipedia*).

Divorce mediation is an option to sit down with your spouse and a mediator to work out arrangements and terms about your financial and family necessities and agreements together in a fair and natural setting. "Mediation is an attempt to remove your divorce from the adversarial arena of the courthouse. Although you can't avoid a lawsuit, you can avoid a bloody battle" (James, *Divorce Mediation Handbook*, 3).

Considering the common knowledge of divorces being stressful, each side is trying their best to make decisions that will help them reach a state of tranquility, having the chance of a setting that allows each individual to express what's important to them along with their goals and needs in a structured manner is important.

"Marriage was an organizing factor in your lives. You and your spouse together made many decisions in particular ways because you were married and shared certain values and expectations. Now those expectations have been turned upside down. You will be negotiating a separation agreement at an emotionally difficult point in your life, and you will [be] required to make decisions without your accustomed underlying rationale. This can be frustrating and confusing" (Butler and Walker, *Divorce Mediation Answer*).

Mediation setting versus litigation helps to make this setting a bit less stressful and out of your direct involvement and control when you are present in every step of the separation process.

"You or your spouse may find that feelings of anxiety over the potential loss of financial security, extended family, home, and friends have a quality more like childhood panic than adult concern, because these losses represent a temporary loss of the 'self' with which you have become comfortable. There may be feeling of betrayal, rage or helplessness. If the two of you become involved in an adversarial process. These feelings may be intensified because you will be dependent on your lawyers strategizing" (Butler and Walker, *Divorce Mediation Answer*).

When being represented by two lawyers in a divorce, you become another one of the many cases they represent every day. The lawyers' approach is by resolving the matter by generalizing background information they have and representing their client. In comparison, mediation makes the case more personalized to each individual, allowing them to speak for themselves considering all their history and knowledge regarding the divorce and future goals.

"A mediator understands this state of mind and will keep the negotiations nonconfrontational and structured. With your mediator's assistance, you will both be able to speak for yourselves and plan your individual future" (Butler and Walker, *Divorce Mediation Answer*).

CHAPTER 2

The Benefits of Mediation in Divorce

With mediation, we have changed the way we solve disputes. When we are using mediation for divorce, we are using many benefits, which the traditional divorce does not offer. Here is a list of these benefits:

1. My opinion matters. Issues that are more sensitive to me. Most people feel there are so many things that are important to them that no one knows or maybe no one cares to know. In mediation, you are able to express your opinion here and now and make sure you are being heard.

   Depending on each individual, there are different things that are important to them that take priority in their life. For example, deciding what each of the children needs, depending on their age and education, are being met better by the mother or the father, which one has more time and the best support system for raising the child? Having the chance to explain this arrangement to the children should be an important conversation. But instead, I've talked to many couples, and they complain about not understanding some of the terminologies that their lawyers use. They are not sure if what they are receiving in their settlement is the same as what they were asking from their divorce attorney. We all like to have our opinion heard, that is why we express it, so having my opinion changed to a terminology that is new to me may not be the same as my opinion for me means not only my concerns aren't heard, but I also feel dissatisfied with the process that is out of touch and out of my control.

2. Speed. I can save time by communicating with my mediator and getting solutions much faster. When I attend a mediation session, I am able to express my opinion and hear my spouse's response to that and be able to get to a faster conclusion. In comparison, having to talk to my attorney and have him talk to my spouse's attorney and then contact my spouse to get an answer back from him and finally back to me, this process sometimes takes days for a conclusion on a simple offer or question.

3. Control. I no longer feel that I have lost control of the divorce process. I am always involved. I can express my priorities here and now, and I am able to control what kind of result I am willing to leave with to make sure it fits my life instead of being told this is what you are being offered, and if we go back to negotiate, you will lose time and money, and most importantly, you have to live with the unknown for a few extra days. Many people in the process of a divorce just make agreements to get rid of the stress and agony that they are so tired of dealing with. Then after the divorce, they ask themselves, Why did I agree on this issue? Only if I had a little more money or patience, I would have done things differently.

4. Educating ourselves. When I am involved in every step of my divorce process, I am more educated about the way the process works, and therefore, I won't have many misunderstandings that many people deal with. Many times, after people had gotten a divorce for the first time in their life, they just realize the dos and don'ts of getting a divorce. The main reason is they are pretty much hands-off with the process and they just hear things from their attorneys over the phone and then they just meet them to sign the papers. When I am new to a process, I am much better off being involved step by step and learning the dos and don'ts now, then I am able to ask more questions and learn about the consequences of every decision now. This will affect the way I negotiate, and I am able to better prioritize my needs rather than insisting on my wants when I am giving up my needs.

5. Mediation is less expensive. Time is money. When you are using the traditional divorce with lawyers and lawsuits, the time it takes is a minimum of four to six months on a simple case, and after that, the more it stretches. You are paying for it with your money and emotions. A traditional divorce in my state may cost anywhere from $5,000 to $20,000 for a basic divorce, according to the law office of Paul G. Dell in McKinney, Texas.

Mediation, for the same type of basic divorce, may not exceed $3,500. Mediation sessions are scheduled with both parties present and with the help of a mediator getting to an immediate conclusion. In the traditional approach with the lawyers, each and every offer needs to be purposeful to both their lawyers and pay for their time to get to the conclusion and you pay for that time after your retainer is used. Of course, the more factors involved—such as children, assets, debts, pets, 401(k)—the more you pay for all these negotiations and the way the lawyers approach it at your expense. It is not surprising to see the expense for these negotiations may come out more than what they thought the issue was worth.

CHAPTER 3

What Does Mediation and the Mediator Do

A divorce mediator provides a fair and sensible setting for the clients to talk about the unique issues they are experiencing and going to be concerned with and provides options to develop alternatives that address those options as much as possible.

"Divorce mediation clients soon learn that there are wide varieties of financial and parenting resolutions that could be incorporated into their divorce decree. Mediation clients are encouraged to focus on many possible alternatives. This is quite different from the focus developed by the clients who choose to litigate their cases in the courts. Litigants tend to focus on developing the best possible resolution for themselves and to focus all of their attention and legal fees on getting exactly that" (Ora Schwartzberg, Divorce Mediation from the Inside Out, 21).

An experienced mediator helps you learn the possibilities about the way you can get a divorce. Possibilities mean options to decide what kind of divorce fits your relationship, and the mediator helps you customize that to fit your life. I call this the art of how to get a divorce. Only a professional mediator may have the tools and knowledge to help you get this customized fit and have your best interest in mind when tailoring every section and every cut of tailoring your situation. But in a traditional divorce, someone else is using a set model for your divorce or gives you different options of divorce models available for you to choose one over another. It is the difference between going to a department store and picking the wardrobe that fits you best and going to your tailor and custom-fitting a personal wardrobe for you. This is essentially the main difference between traditional divorce and divorce with mediation. Of course, this type of divorce is not something that works for everyone, especially for those with lots of assets or liabilities, as customized tailoring is not something that works for everyone, except this type of customizing costs less than the traditional way.

A divorce can take years—and cost a small fortune— to resolve. The task of negotiating child and spousal support, dividing property and other possessions, and establishing child-custody arrangements can be overwhelming, especially when the principals are barely speaking to each other. In the worst-case scenario, separating spouses hire cutthroat lawyers to make rigid (and sometimes outrageous) demands, the two sides dig in, a judge takes over, and animosity reaches a fever pitch.

Divorce mediation would seem to offer a more peaceful alternative to traditional adversarial divorce negotiations. And, indeed, by drawing on proven mediation strategies, divorce mediation has been found to achieve higher settlement rates than

litigation. (www.pon.harvard.edu/daily/mediation/
what-is-divorce-mediation/)

Getting divorced is like getting on a roller coaster for the first time without knowing what is going to happen next. This roller coaster comes with a start that feeds into an up-and-down journey with an unpredictable finish. Going to a mediator is like going to someone who has helped several people through their roller-coaster rides and has experienced the ups and downs. A mediator can provide a general idea of what you need to get yourself ready for the ride. Spending time and thinking about the things that are most important to you prior to your session with a mediator is essential. When you are already in agreement with your mediator and have communicated, you're able to come to a divorce agreement much faster and spend less time on issues that aren't your immediate needs.

A mediator has helped many people who have reached a dead end in their relationship find the best possible way to get out of that dead end, so he or she has a lot of knowledge and experience on options that help the sides go past the disagreements and think about the future and help think about their own future and the decisions they are making today that is going to help them have a better result in their agreement to live a better life in the future.

One of the main reasons why lots of relationships get to this dead end is the lack of communication. They either did not know how to communicate with each other or they did not communicate at all. So the disputes were always there without any solution; but with the help of a mediator, they will find solutions, they will realize they have a chance to have their opinions heard, and the mediators explain to them how to ask for and negotiate all things that are so important to them. The main reason lots of new divorces get to mediation is that more and more people realize a mediator helps both sides concentrate on the divorce and what helps them to finalize it instead of all the side issues that come along with the whole process of losing an old life and life partner and how to deal with the new transition at the start of a new life. The faster and more practical one can go through this process helps one have a new, better start at life with a better understanding of what has happened that one has to get divorced and how one can get myself back on the right track, so one doesn't lose any more emotion, time, and money and life altogether.

How does the quality of divorce agreements facilitated by mediators compare with that of agreements obtained through lawyers? Researcher Rachid Baitar of the Catholic University of Leuven and Ghent University in Belgium and his colleagues examined this question in a 2012 study of 469 divorcing individuals in Belgium. About half of the participants reported experiencing a high level of conflict with their spouse before the divorce; for others, conflict was less intense or minimal.

In the study, a mediator assisted 30% of participants in reaching agreement; the other 70% of participants were helped by a lawyer. As compared with participants who engaged in litigation, participants who engaged in divorce mediation reported reaching higher-quality agreements, as measured by how tailored, fair, comprehensive, and clear those agreements were. Notably, the results of Baitar and his colleagues' study need to be qualified by the fact that the participants themselves chose whether to mediate or litigate. It could be that those who chose divorce mediation entered into the process with a less combative attitude than those who chose litigation, a difference that would weaken the study's results.

In addition to looking at whether the divorces were mediated or litigated, the researchers examined the negotiating style of the mediators and lawyers involved. In a facilitative mediation, the mediator focuses on helping parties carry out a smooth, open conversation; in an evaluative mediation, the mediator may also evaluate parties' positions and even propose a settlement. Many divorce attorneys have begun to adopt a more facilitative approach—for example, by trying to de-escalate conflict and improve the quality of the relationship between the divorcing spouses.

Study participants whose mediator or lawyer took a facilitative approach to the negotiation, as measured by their tendency to engage in problem-solving behaviors and help their clients focus on interests, generally reported high-quality outcomes. (www.pon.harvard. edu/daily/mediation/what-is-divorce-mediation)

CHAPTER 4

The Process of Divorce Mediation

Now we may review the process of getting a divorce. The first step is deciding to get a mediated divorce when you have decided and know you are going to go forward with your decision. Then you search for the right firm to help you. In the beginning, you and your husband or wife may not agree on mediation, so you need to take the first step by yourself to make a few calls and even go on a few interviews to educate yourself about the mediation process and find answers to some of the questions that you and your spouse may have. Plus, depending on the firm that you contact, you will be provided with materials that explain the basic process of mediation they practice, and then you have the option of how to approach this whole experience and how to be dealing with it. Here are some of the most important benefits that you will receive by going through mediation that you can also share with your spouse. I have gathered two different formats from different sources to make it easy for you to compare and understand the mediation benefits.

Mediation versus Litigation

For the majority of cases, we can compare the process of mediation to the litigation process as far as terms, time, cost, and self-involvement. The ability to be self-involved helps the individual gain control over the process rather than having them feel as though they are being condemned to have no control over the process and outcome.

In many cases, the unexpected mental stress is so out of control that it causes a new mental condition or financial issues in people's lives that is hard to recover from.

That is why I'm using a comparison between mediation versus litigation, so we can understand both processes better.

Getting Divorced: Mediation vs. Litigation

Here are ten reasons more and more people are becoming familiar with divorce mediation.

1. Money and cost

   After finding the right mediation firm, you and your spouse meet together with one divorce mediator. Commonly, you share the cost, which is usually between $3,000 and $6,000 in total, depending on your family size and assets. If you were to hire separate attorneys to represent you in the divorce, you would each typically pay a retainer of $1,000 to $5,000 just to get started. In Texas, a typical litigated divorce costs about $20,000 to $40,000.

2. Your opinion matter and you have control

   In divorce mediation, your opinion is discussed. You both

control how quickly or slowly decisions are made, when the divorce decree is filed, and what the terms of the divorce will be. Each step is by agreement, in contrast to the adversarial process in which attorneys negotiate on your behalf and set court dates and judges make decisions within a limited time and information.

3. The paperwork is done for you

When individuals try to do their own divorce without the right information and knowledge, they run into difficulties, trying to understand the laws and then the confusing paperwork involved. The mediator, who is also an attorney, can prepare and file all of the paperwork for you.

4. Children and the effect on them

Children probably receive the worst effects of a divorce. The conflict between the parents is tremendous for children. Parents have the opportunity to work together and make adult decisions, not put them in the middle of the battle.

5. Less stress

It is important to keep in mind the way your marriage ends will significantly affect the way you approach your future relationships. Using a mediator to help facilitate communication and to make important decisions makes it more satisfactory, and it is much easier to move forward and accept the past, rather than turning the old, stressful, and angry times into an expensive court battle.

6. You always have the option to go to court

By using divorce mediation, you do not give up your right to go to court. If you are not satisfied in mediation, you can stop at any time and go ahead to retain a separate attorney and have the judge make the decision on unresolved issues.

7. You won't receive legal advice but legal information

In divorce mediation with your mediator, who is also an attorney, you will both be provided with legal information to help you make decisions about what is fair. An attorney acting in the role of a mediator cannot give either of you legal advice, but they can share general knowledge of how a court might address the issues in similar cases.

8. Emotions and anger

In your divorce process, you want to be heard and understood in your own words. This may be difficult. Anger and emotions may be unintentionally triggered. An experienced mediator can help you address emotions without allowing such feelings to dominate your decision-making process or affect the other party's decision-making. In court, emotions often drive the case, and the cost, more than any legal issue.

9. Confidentiality

All discussions and tentative agreements are confidential in divorce mediation.

Confidentiality makes it easier for you to make offers and consider alternatives without having everything completely planned out. Many times you arrive at a new arrangement neither of you had previously considered.

10. It helps to build a positive outlook

By coming together in mediation, the mediator will encourage you both to find a common ground for making agreements. The focus is on important future decisions, not memories.

Here we have mediation versus litigation according to the National Conflict Resolution Center (www.ncrconline.com/divorce/mediationvslitigation).

*Cost

Mediation rate $300/hour for mediation time (shared between parties)

Document preparation fees: $1,800–$2,500.

Average total: $2,500–$5,000

Litigation:

The average rate for attorneys $300–$ 350/hour each

Average total: $20,000 per person

*Time

The time involved in mediation, average time: 3–6 months (depends on needs of couple)

Average time with attorneys: 2 years (depends on court schedule)

*Process

In mediation: The tone of the process is businesslike but informal

With attorneys: Formal, adversarial role of the law

*Legal Advice

Information provided by mediator but no legal advice given

Legal information and legal advice given by counsel

*Children

In mediation: Impact on children—children's interests are central to decision making; interim agreements possible

Attorneys: Children often become pawns in the battle between the spouses

Voluntary compliance with child support agreements, the nationwide figures are around 80%

With attorneys: Nationwide figures are around 40%

*Emotional

In mediation: Emotional cost to parties, allows for healthy airing of diverse views and emotions, more comfortable, cooperative.

Increases anxiety and stress with attorneys: Little opportunity to address concerns; stressful, adversarial

*Communication

In mediation: Impact on communication, promotes improved communication, sets the stage for joint decision-making, encourages personal responsibility

With attorneys: Discourages communication, sets the stage for future disagreements and possible court appearances

*Decisions

In mediation: Decision Making Clients make their own decisions

With attorneys: Third parties (judges and attorneys) make decisions

*Confidentiality

In mediation: Confidentiality Discussions and financial information are confidential, usually no court appearances

With attorneys: Hearings are open to the public; financial information is part of the public record (several court appearances)

By knowing the benefits of mediation and evaluating your options, it is much easier to make a decision on what is the most suitable for your life, and knowing this information helps you have an outlook of what you need to get yourself ready for and when you are ready it helps to interview mediators and make a decision about who you feel comfortable with.

Keep in mind there are special cases, such as physical and mental abuse, addiction of one or both parties, criminal activity, and personal mental health problem issues that would make it very difficult to use mediation for divorce, so litigation is the primary choice of the parties to keep all legal and personal relationships under control and according to the law of the state where the divorce is taking place.

CHAPTER 5

Initial Interview

After making a decision to use mediation for your divorce, you have to make a checklist and make yourself ready for the initial interview. You need to pay close attention to what a qualified mediator should be able to offer in mediation.

"A good mediator puts forth proposals that meet the interests of both parties. They don't respond to irrational behavior, and they don't make unilateral concessions in an effort to win one party over the other. Doing so will only encourage them to continue their bad behavior. After each meeting, they summarize what transpired in writing and distribute copies to everyone involved" (www.pon. harvard.edu/daily/mediation/dispute-resolution-how-mediation).

One of the most important things that this initial interview should provide for you is the realization of how this process works. The mediator will show you how to prioritize and explain the process in sections, so you are not overwhelmed with the decisions all at once, and then you make decisions step by step. This is what you need to be told, and if not, this is how your questions should be asked!

- What are the steps in your process of mediation?

- How much would it cost for each or both sides?
- How do we get better prepared for our sessions?

With an experienced mediator, the process should be explained, how you are going to be guided into generating options and analyzing and evaluating proposals so without deviation you arrive at the settlement.

> Getting divorced is like driving on the freeway in a fog so thick that you cannot see more than a few feet in any direction. The decisions you make are crucial, a mistake can cause serious damage.

> The mediator is like a driving instructor helping you navigate. Standing outside the fog, he watches your progress, points out when you are about to go off-road or run into another car, and guides you through the treacherous turns on your way home. (James, *Divorce Mediation Handbook*, 41)

The divorce process is so unknown to many people that it makes them take extreme measures, which are not necessary if you are well educated about the process but not having the knowledge, it makes people think of the worst disasters when they are about to face getting a divorce. They either try to avoid it as much and as long as they can, or they get ready for the worst disaster they may have to experience. I think this is the result of not having the right information.

At the initial interview, both spouses may be present, and after asking the general questions, an initial appointment is set, which both spouses will attend. Both spouses may mention what are the most important concerns, what are the most important factors in their lives to talk about, and the needs to be protected or dealt with. After the main factors are disclosed, they are informed how they may prioritize each one. After prioritizing, the general goals of the parties are discussed; that would be the rules and guidelines by which mediation would be guided initially, and then other concerns may rise, which would be addressed and discussed one by one, so the parties may reach an agreement with the time needed.

These rules would be between the parties themselves, as well as the mediator. Copies are then made, reviewed, and signed.

Agreement to Mediate and the Rules

Definition of Mediation. Mediation is a process during which an impartial person, the mediator, facilitates communication between the parties to promote reconciliation, settlement, or understanding between them.

Scope of the Mediator. The mediator may suggest ways of resolving the dispute but may not impose the mediator's own judgment on the issues for that of the parties. The mediator shall act as an advocate for a resolution and shall use the mediator's best efforts to assist the parties in reaching a mutually acceptable settlement. The mediator may not give any legal advice to either party. In addition, the mediator may not meet with or speak to either party outside the presence of their attorney.

Agreement of the Parties. Whenever the parties have agreed to the mediation, they shall be deemed to have made these rules, as amended and in effect as of the date of the submission of the dispute, a part of their agreement to mediate.

Consent to the Mediator. The parties' consent to the appointment of the individual named as mediator in their case as evidenced by their signatures herein.

Conditions Precedent to Serving as a Mediator. The mediator shall not serve as a mediator in any dispute in which he has any financial or personal interest in the result of the mediation. Prior to accepting an appointment, the mediator shall disclose any circumstances likely to create a presumption of bias or prevent a prompt meeting with the parties. If the parties disagree about whether the mediator shall serve, the mediator shall not serve.

Authority of the Mediator. The mediator does not have the authority to decide any issue for the parties but will attempt to facilitate the voluntary resolution of the dispute by the parties. The mediator is authorized to conduct joint and separate meetings with the parties and offers suggestions to help the parties achieve a settlement. If necessary, the mediator may also obtain expert advice concerning technical aspects of the dispute, provided that the parties agree and assume the expenses of obtaining the advice. Arrangements for obtaining such advice shall be made by the mediator or the parties, as the mediator shall determine.

Commitment to Participate in Good Faith. While no one is asked to commit to settling the case in advance of mediation, all parties commit to participate in the proceedings in good faith with the intention to settle, if at all possible.

Parties Responsible for Negotiating Their Settlement. The parties understand that the mediator will not and cannot impose a settlement in their case and agree that they are responsible for negotiating a settlement acceptable to them. The mediator, as an advocate for settlement, will use every effort to facilitate the negotiations of the parties. The Mediator does not warrant or represent that settlement will result from the mediation process.

Authority to Settle. The parties must have the authority to settle, and all persons necessary to the decision to settle shall be present.

Time and Place of Mediation. The mediator shall fix the time of each mediation session. The mediation shall be held at the office of the mediator or at any other convenient location agreeable to the mediator and the parties, as the mediator shall determine.

Identification of the Matter in Dispute. Before the first scheduled mediation session, each party shall provide the mediator with a completed and signed information sheet and consent to the mediation on the form furnished by the mediator, setting forth the party's position with regard to the issues that need to be resolved. At or before the first session, the parties will be expected to produce all information reasonably required for the mediator to understand the issues and the dispute. The mediator may require any party to supplement the information.

Privacy. Mediation sessions are private. The parties and their attorneys must attend the mediation sessions. Other persons may attend only with the permission of the parties and with the consent of the mediator.

Confidentiality. Confidential information disclosed to a mediator by the parties or by witnesses in the course of the mediation shall not be divulged by the mediator. In certain instances, applicable law may require a disclosure of information revealed in the mediation process. For example, the Texas Family Code's Section 261.101 may require a mediator to disclose child abuse or neglect to the appropriate authorities. If confidential information is disclosed that is required to be reported, the mediator will advise the parties that disclosure is required and will be made.

All records, reports, or other documents received by a mediator while serving in that capacity shall be confidential. The mediator shall not be compelled to divulge such records or to testify in regard to the mediation in any adversarial proceeding or judicial forum. Any party that violates this agreement shall pay all the fees and expenses of the mediator and other parties, including reasonable attorney's fees incurred in opposing the efforts to compel testimony or records from the mediator.

The parties shall maintain the confidentiality of the mediation and shall not rely on or introduce as evidence in any arbitration, judicial or other proceedings, (a) views expressed or suggestions made by another party with respect to a possible settlement of the dispute, (b) admissions made by another party in the course of the mediation proceedings, (c) proposals made or views expressed by the mediator, or (d) the fact that another party had or had not indicated a willingness to accept a proposal for settlement made by the Mediator.

No Record of Session. There shall be no electronic or stenographic record of any mediation session.

No Service of Process at or Near the Site of the Mediation Session. No subpoena, summons, complaints, citations, writs, or other processes may be served at or near the site of any mediation session or upon any person entering, attending, or leaving the mediation session.

Termination of Mediation. The mediation shall be concluded (a) by the execution of a settlement agreement by the parties; (b) by the declaration of the mediator to the effect that further efforts at mediation are no longer worthwhile; or (c) after the completion of one full mediation session, by a written declaration or verbal declaration of a party or parties to the effect that the mediation proceedings are terminated.

Exclusion of Liability. The mediator is not a necessary or proper party in judicial proceedings relating to the mediation. Neither the mediator nor any law firm employing the mediator shall be liable to any party for any act or omission in connection with any mediation conducted or settlement reached under these rules.

Interpretation and Application of the Rules. The mediator shall interpret and apply these rules.

Fees and Expenses. The mediator's daily fee shall be agreed upon before mediation and shall be paid in advance of each mediation day. The expenses of witnesses for either side shall be paid by the party producing the witnesses. All other expenses of the mediation, including fees and expenses of the mediator and the expenses of any witness and the cost of any proofs or expert advice produced at the direct request of the mediator, shall be borne equally by the parties unless they agree otherwise.

As per my signature below, I have read and understand the above rules for family mediation and release the mediator, Roy Ghassemi, from any and all liability in connection with this mediation.

SIGNED on _____,

_____   _____
Petitioner   Respondent

The mediator will ask the clients for certain basic information at this initial meeting, a personal section and financial statement section which is provided to your CPA to file your taxes. It will consist of bringing in certain information and documentation to the next meeting. Having a list of assets, credit cards, memberships, etc., here is a sample form to show how the list can be organized.

Full disclosure and verification of all figures that are submitted is the optimum situation prior to the commencement of the mediation. The participants are to provide the following documentation and information:

❑ 1. Copies of three years of tax returns, including schedules and forms, for past three years (each of you should also have a copy)

❑ 2. Most recent pay statement(s)

❑ 3. Most recent brokerage firm(s) statement(s)

❑ 4. Most recent bank account statement(s), including savings, checking, and CDs

❑ 5. Most recent statement from all creditors

❑ 6. Payoff and blue book values on motor vehicles and trailers (blue book figures usually available from your bank)

❑ 7. Statement from your employer(s) regarding pensions, profit sharing, stock options; we also need a copy of your benefit explanation booklet

❑ 8. Year-end statement from the lender who has your mortgage

❑ 9. Most recent statement from employer(s) company benefits and company benefits booklet

❑ 10. Partnerships, closely-held business or professional practice

❑ 11. Copies of reports from limited partnerships, contracts, etc.

❑ 12. Current budget plus post-divorce budget

❑ 13. Prenuptial and postnuptial

❑ 14. Insurance policy

❑ 15. Anything else that will assist in assigning value to your assets and liabilities

There are some sample forms that I have prepared that you may use to gather some basic information about yourself before the interview because some of the answers to the questions you may have include the list of information you bring with you.

Real Estate

Location of Property: _____

Title in name(s) of: _____

Date Purchased: _____ Purchase price: $_____

Lender: _____ Down payment: $_____

_____ Mortgage: $_____

Account Number: _____ Balance owing : $_____

Length of mortgage: _____ Interest rate: _____

Vehicles

Make: _____

Model: _____

Year: _____

Current value: _____

Amount owed: _____

Lender: _____

Accounts Receivable

Name	Terms	Original Amount/Balance	Date of last payment

Other Assets

Indicate if you are self-employed and attach your balance sheet and profit and loss statements for the past three years.

Item	Price paid	Value	Amount owed against

Household Items

Item	Price Paid	Value	Amount owed against

Jewelry

Item	Price paid	Value	Amount owed against

Retirement Plans

Employment, IRA, SEP-IRA, 401(k), KEOGH, ESOP, ETC.

Date of vesting	Type of plan	Investment contribution	Vested value

Budget Blueprint

Expense	Weekly	Per Paycheck	Monthly	Quarterly	Yearly	Goals
Rent or mortgage						
Utilities						
Heat						
Property taxes						
Water						
Garden supplies						
Telephone						
Property insurance						
Maintenance/cleaning						
Garbage collection						
Condominium fees						
Car payment						
Gasoline						
Maintenance/cleaning						
License						
Insurance						
Bus/taxi/tolls/parking						
Groceries						
Delivered goods						
Snacks						
Work lunches						
School lunches						

Expense	Weekly	Per Paycheck	Monthly	Quarterly	Yearly	Goals
Personal						
Spouse						
Children						
Maintenance/cleaning						
Vacations						
Meals out						
Movies/plays/music						
Spectator sports						
Sports equipment						
Television/cable						
Credit union (%)						
Education (%)						
Co. savings plan (%)						
IRA (%)						
Other (%)						
Medications						
Insurance						
Doctor						
Dentist						
Exercise class/equip.						
Lessons						

Expense	Weekly	Per Paycheck	Monthly	Quarterly	Yearly	Goals
Tuition						
Books/papers						
Supplies						
Life insurance						
Legal						
Child care						
Allowances						
Gifts						
Pets (food, medical)						
Church/synagogue						
Political						
Charitable						
Other						
Barber/beauty shop						
Toiletries						
Postage						
Tobacco						
Alcohol						
Other						
Credit union (%)						
Credit card (%)						
Credit card 2 (%)						

Expense	Weekly	Per Paycheck	Monthly	Quarterly	Yearly	Goals
Department store (%)						
Student loan (%)						
Other (%)						
Other (%)						
Union dues						
Taxes: Social security						
Federal income						
State income						
Local income						
Non-reimbursed business expenses						
Other						
Other						
Total outgoing:						

Income						
Paycheck						
Paycheck						
Dividends						
Interest						
Social security						
Pension						
Gifts						
Other						
Total income:						

They can have time to ask the more personal questions if they wish to make sure mediation is right for them, questions like if they are allowed to have their attorney involved in the process, and how involved the attorneys could be.

CHAPTER 6

When to Have Attorneys Involved

Understanding your legal rights is essential to your divorce process, and mediators may be able to provide information regarding your rights, but as far as recommendation and legal advice, that is something that you need to consult your attorney for. Before during and at the end of mediation, before signing the final papers, you may consult your attorney to receive recommendations on legal issues.

"What can a lawyer do that your mediator cannot? Your mediator's job is to help you and your spouse reach an agreement, but because he's neutral, he cannot advise you as to whether your agreement is wise. Remember that, in driving through the fog. You choose your destination, your mediator merely helps you get there. Your lawyer, on the other hand, helps you think clearly about your destination" (James, *Divorce Mediation Handbook*, 47).

They may offer you answers to your legal questions to help you understand how the law applies to your divorce.

Your attorney's job is not to make you ready for a war with your spouse and drag the process longer than it needs to. His job is to give you support on the legal issues that you are concerned with, and you can make the best intelligent decision that fits your life in mediation.

You may also have your attorney present in mediation when you have decided on using mediation for your divorce. Ask your attorney to be present to help you understand your rights and also help you negotiate better or have a stronger position. Your attorney may help you as your coach with suggestions and support and generally give you a better level of confidence when present.

Of course, when one side asks for their attorney to be present in the mediation, it is also the other party's right to have their attorney present as well. Therefore, it is important to use the attorneys' help when they can support the process. They understand, that is why you need their help there and not make things more complicated or aggravate the other spouse. It is very important that you check on the attorney's qualification in family law. It is pretty obvious that a tax attorney would not be a good choice for divorce mediation, but it's not impossible to see one in a divorce mediation when they should not be there in the first place.

We had a case of divorce with the Smith family a while back. Mr. Smith had his cousin's husband, who is a tax attorney, present for advice and support. From the beginning, he was advising Mr. Smith about the tax complications of giving the wife the house and how it affects the tax returns in future years. Even though they were saying we can sell the house and not have to deal with the future tax complication, he would bring up another complication regarding the future tax dilemma. So I had to explain that every time there is a divorce, there are tax issues for the first couple of years that the husband and wife will be facing, and that is until everything is sold, and then file taxes separately. That is part of the divorce process. There is no way to avoid that. If an attorney with a family law background was present, he would have been familiar with the process, and we did not have to spend a couple of hours on an issue that was normal for other family law attorneys in mediation.

Another important point about choosing an attorney to be present in mediation is to ask one that believes in mediation. There are attorneys who only believe in litigation to be comfortable in protecting their clients' legal rights. Even though they may have been in many mediations before, they are not convinced the client's rights can be protected in mediation, and their rights may only be protected through an adversarial process. Therefore, it is important that you ask an attorney who believes in mediation for the divorce and is familiar with the process. When talking about mediation with an attorney, you can simply watch his reaction. You would see how he responds to your questions and whether he is comfortable responding to you in a common manner. They would show it by explaining past experiences or positive recommendations that they share with you. Or they would try to cut you short and tell you about the drawbacks and all the legal benefits that you may not understand at this time and you don't realize unless he or another attorney represents you to protect your rights. Of course, if that were the case, we did not have mediation as part of our legal system now, and it is proven to be so effective that is being used more and more every day, especially in divorce.

CHAPTER 7

Children in Divorce

When people are getting a divorce, they are so angry that they give little thought to the relationship the children have with the other parent. They are so occupied with getting the sinking ship to shore that they don't consider the importance of the essential fact they leave behind. They are usually focused on getting themselves out of the situation they are in and even care for the children the best way they know how. But the feeling of anger, which they carry, comes out by using the children. Sometimes they want to punish the spouse by limiting the time they spend with children, and this way, they feel satisfied by revenge.

But one cannot forget that every child needs the best possible care that both parents can give, especially during and after the divorce is final. If one parent is diminishing the character of the other parent, directly or indirectly, they are affecting the care the other parent is able to provide to that child.

Children's characters are built on care, attention, and time provided by their parents. Unless a parent is clinically or mentally ill, it is necessary to pay attention to the values that parents provide for their children. The upbringing of the child is an important point that is often brought up in mediation that requires the attention of both parents.

A firm stand on different issues, even on time spent with children, is reasonable, but you may also consult with a psychologist about your specific situation to know the outcome of your decision and how firm on each issue you may be. Every future decision you make affects your children.

"Using data from the National Institute of Child Health and Human Development Study of Early Child Care and Youth Development, we examined children's internalizing and externalizing behavior problems from age 5 to 15 years in relation to whether they had experienced a parental divorce. Children from divorced families had more behavior problems compared with a propensity-score-matched sample of children from intact families, according to both teachers and mothers. They exhibited more internalizing and externalizing problems at the first assessment after the parents' separation and at the last available assessment (age 11 years for teacher reports, or 15 years for mother reports). Divorce also predicted both short-term and long-term rank-order increases in behavior problems. Associations between divorce and child behavior problems were moderated by family income (assessed before the divorce) such that children from families with higher incomes prior to the separation had fewer internalizing problems than children from families with lower incomes prior to the separation. Higher levels of pre-divorce maternal sensitivity and child IQ also functioned as protective factors for children of divorce. Mediation analyses showed that children were more likely to exhibit behavior problems after the divorce if their postdivorce home environment was less supportive and stimulating, their mother was less sensitive and more depressed, and their household income was lower. We discuss avenues for intervention, particularly efforts to improve the quality of home environments in divorced families" (Jennifer M. Weaver, et al., "Mediation and moderation of divorce effects on children's behavior problems," *Journal of Family Psychology* 29, no. 1 (2015): 39–48, National Library of Medicine, https://pubmed.ncbi.nlm.nih.gov/25419913/).

You also have to keep in mind that many arrangements that you so insist on having now, if it is not thought well in advance, you may want to change in the near future, so it would be best to make a firm decision on issues that you have knowledge of the outcome, or just take a couple of days and do research on that issue, especially when it concerns the children's lives at different ages.

For example, we all know stability is an important factor in children's lives, but at the same time, being able to balance the time they spend with each parent at different ages is as important.

> Experts disagree on the importance of stability versus large amounts of time with both parents, but they do agree that the need for stability is greater for young children and diminishes as the children grow.
>
> They also agree on the following:
>
> Children need sufficient time with each parent to maintain a healthy relationship with both.
>
> Children need not to spend half their time with each parent, although such division is sometimes desirable.
>
> Children's well-being is affected more by the parents attitudes about sharing custody than by how much time they spend with each parent (assuming that

the children have a base amount of time with each parent). (James, *Divorce Mediation Handbook*, 121)

Keep in mind the life of your children revolves around each one of you as the parent and caregiver, and they care about you both, caring and providing for them. They are living and learning how to behave based on your behavior in general. They especially care to know and to learn how you are behaving toward the other parent. The better we plan this future relationship, as well as the schedules and routines, the easier time you and the children will have in experiencing the new life ahead.

CHAPTER 8

Dos and Don'ts in Mediation

The most important issue to remember during the mediation is to know your needs and necessities ahead of time. The problem that everyone may encounter is usually getting sidetracked and mix the wants with the needs. An experienced mediator's job is to keep the client on the right track, so they don't lose their focus on the needs and allow the personal challenges, or old grudges, get in the way of thinking what they really need to have.

Knowing your priorities in the mediation session is very important. Being prepared to negotiate based on priorities is the center of mediation. Having that list will keep you focused on getting most of your needs.

Not having a list of your priorities means you are not prepared to negotiate or you are not prepared to negotiate based on your needs. This is the way to not to get your needs but also spend an extra amount of time on issues that may not affect you or your children's lives by next year or so. Instead, you spend a lot of energy negotiating it.

Here are some other examples of the dos and don'ts by Sabrina Harrison:

Don'ts

Don't use mediation as a fact-finding mission. Divorce mediation is intended for good-faith interactions where you actually intend to come to an agreement. If you are on an expedition for information, don't waste your time or the mediator's.

Don't come to the mediation with a closed mind. Maybe what you agree to was not originally what you had planned, but if it works, it works. Some of the most interesting cases I have had were when parents came up with their own creative solutions.

Don't try to avoid costs by excluding your divorce attorney. These meetings have legal consequences and ramifications. No, you don't have to bring your lawyer all the time, but make sure they have had a chance to advise you so that you feel comfortable talking about and making decisions about the issues at hand—custody, visitation, child support, spousal support, and your debts and assets.

Don't get in over your head. You don't do yourself any favors by digging into the asset or debt division or retirement accounts if you don't understand the issues. There is no shame in it! You are probably not a lawyer or financial advisor! If you feel over your head, it is a great time to take a break and call your divorce attorney or financial advisor or schedule a meeting with them before your second session in mediation. You want to feel good about your mediation outcomes, and getting help from professionals can go a long way toward this goal.

Dos

Do let a supportive person know when your divorce mediation is so that they can come with you for moral support or be available on the phone. Let your divorce attorney know as well. You may not know if what is being offered is really a good deal, and a mediator cannot advise you about what is in your best interests or give you legal advice.

Do take breaks. You don't win a prize for getting out of the room the fastest. If things are getting tense, take a minute. The divorce mediator will often suggest this, but you have the right to take a break at any time. This device gives everyone a chance to reset, but it also gets you away from the momentum. You are less likely to give things away that actually matter to you if you take a minute. Eat a snack that you planned and packed, call your mom, or call your lawyer. Taking breaks makes sure that you can feel good about the agreement that you are making and aren't just rushing to get away from the other party.

Do schedule a second mediation session if you need to. Again, no one wins the prize for getting it done the fastest. Remember that you will have to live with this legally binding document regarding your children's custody, visitation, child support, or debt and assets division for a long time. If your support person isn't available, the other party isn't prepared, you come up with a draft document that you need your lawyer to review, you need to pick up a child or get back or work, and schedule another session to finish. (Sabrina Harrison, Jonathan M. Murdoch-Kitt website, murdochkittlaw.com/)

Another common example of do's and don'ts relates to negotiating over children.

For most individuals, negotiating over children is difficult. The power struggle starts with talking about child custody or child support. But as long as both sides are prepared for the actual child's needs and priorities, it will reduce the tension between the parents. They can always share the list they have prepared in mediation and try to work with the priorities. Without that list, power struggles start and both sides want to win the challenge, considering the challenge itself is only 50 percent benefiting the child, but mainly about who can have more control.

It is obvious that when a couple wants to talk about the best mental future for the child, they need to consult a child psychologist, and after that, they come up with the approximate amount of time and allowance that needs to be provided to the main caretaker. By doing this, we can eliminate a lot of the arguments and power struggles that are repeatedly happening over the child's welfare and future.

Besides the fights over the assets in the divorce, child custody and child support are the next most expensive challenges a couple spends money on with their attorneys to get what they want and not necessarily what their child needs. So any time you feel you are finding yourself with such a challenge that you are not even sure of the benefits, you simply need to step away from the negotiation table for a few minutes or just leave that subject for a later time to review your list of priorities.

You also want to think when you are walking away from the mediation and the negotiation table that you have not missed anything and you don't have any regrets that you wish to have changed or revised. With this in mind, you are always thinking about the outcome of your mediation and how your divorce settlement is going to look.

CHAPTER 9

Mediation Settlement Agreement (MSA)

The mediated settlement agreement (MSA) is exactly what it sounds like. It is an agreement reached through the process of mediation by both spouses. The agreement may address issues of the suit before the court, including property division, spousal maintenance, child support, child custody, and more. Mediation is where most Texas divorces are actually resolved. An agreement reached through mediation is one of the parties' own making. That means both spouses agreed to the terms of the MSA, rather than having an unfamiliar third party (i.e., a judge) dictate the terms of a decree for them. A further benefit of the MSA is that once it is reached, i.e. the parties and their attorneys sign off on it, the parties are entitled to a judgment from the court. After the MSA is agreed to, then the parties must then take the further step of enshrining that agreement in a decree.

Even for spouses who find they disagree on these major issues, sometimes vehemently so, negotiating a mediated settlement agreement between the two of them without the involvement of the court often is a much more desirable, not to mention less stressful, option. It is an instrument of their own making.

The Divorce Decree

"The mediated settlement agreement, while a written document worked out between the two spouses, still needs to be approved by the court in the form of a decree. The MSA alone does not dissolve a marriage. The decree is a court order that identifies the parties, any children under the age of eighteen (or not otherwise emancipated), and articulates the terms of the agreement (the MSA) reached between the two of them" ("Difference Between Mediated Settlement Agreement vs. Divorce Decree," OndaFamilyLaw.com).

The mediation is all about reaching your agreement to be put in a settlement statement. That is called the mediation settlement agreement. The mediator's job is to have your agreements put in writing and prepared to have them signed by all parties. Then you take it to court to be approved to become a divorce decree. The final settlement is what you are left with when mediation is over. According to the municipal system of the place you reside, the settlement has to include the agreement and will include certain information that will help you know and have guidelines. Your mediator may prepare a draft of the final and present it to you to have your attorney write the final mediation settlement agreement, or he can write the draft himself. The main thing to consider in this final process is the difference between the two processes.

If the mediator prepares a draft for your attorney to draw the mediation settlement agreement, the attorney may have some questions, instead of concentrating on the draft they are preparing and start a new negotiation. But if the mediator is preparing the final mediation settlement agreement, he is a mutual third party and has been involved in every session of the mediation, knows well the concerns of both parties, and without being biased, will draft the settlement. Then an attorney, who is not involved with either one of the parties, will review the draft and finalize it. In some cases, such as mediation with a psychologist mediator, they may have an unbiased attorney present in the last mediation session, so they can have more knowledge of the parties and their needs to draft the mediation settlement agreement to present to the court.

That also allows parties to ask any final questions about the mediation settlement agreement as well.

Sample Form,

NO. _____

IN THE MATTER OF	* IN THE DISTRICT COURT
THE MARRIAGE OF	*
*	
HWG	*
*	
AND	*
*	
ASG	*
*_____ JUDICIAL DISTRICT	
IN THE INTEREST OF	*
*	
CHILD1 and	*
CHILD2	*
MINOR CHILDREN	* ....COUNTY, TEXAS

MEDIATION SETTLEMENT AGREEMENT

The parties to this action are: HWG (hereinafter sometimes referred to as "Husband" or "Father" and ASG (hereinafter sometimes referred to as "Wife" or "Mother").

The parties have reached the following agreements in mediation and pursuant to Rule 11 Texas Rules of Civil Procedure agree and stipulate that this agreement shall be presented to the Court as evidence of their agreement and that they intend to be bound by said agreement pursuant to Sec. 154.071, Texas Practice and Remedies Code.

The parties agree that either party shall be entitled to a final divorce decree that shall reflect each term of this agreement. In the event that either party obstructs the entry of a final judgment consistent with this agreement, the prevailing party on a motion for summary judgment, motion for entry or other similar action shall be entitled to reimbursement of that party's reasonable attorney fees and costs associated with such action.

The parties agree that the final divorce decree and all closing documents incorporating this mediated settlement agreement shall follow the forms contained in the Texas Family Practice Manual. Prior to filing any motions with the court the parties further agree that they shall attempt to resolve any disputes regarding the interpretation or performance of this agreement, including the necessity and form of closing documents, through a conference call with the mediator and where possible by reference to the practice manual forms.

Pursuant to Sec. 6.602 and Sec.153.0071, Texas Family Code, this Mediation Settlement Agreement is not subject to revocation.

The children the subject of this agreement is/are:

NAME: CHILD1

SEX: Female

BIRTH DATE: _____

NAME: CHILD2

SEX: Female

BIRTH DATE: _____

Conservatorship

_____ and _____ shall be appointed Joint Managing Conservators of the child(ren).

The exclusive right to designate the primary residence of the child(ren) shall be awarded to: _____ without geographical restriction _____ restricted to _____

Husband shall have the following rights and duties checked below:

_____ the right to receive information from any other conservator of the child concerning the health education, and welfare of the child;

_____ the right to confer with the other parent to the extent possible before making a decision concerning the health education and welfare of the child;

_____ the right of access to medical, dental, psychological, and educational records of the child;

_____ the right to consult with a physician, dentist, or psychologist of the child;

_____ the right to consult with school officials concerning the child's welfare and educational status, including school activities;

____ the right to attend school activities;

____ the right to be designated on the child's records as a person to be notified in case of an emergency.

____ the right to consent to medical, dental, and surgical treatment during an emergency involving an immediate danger to the health and safety of the child;

____ the right to manage the estate of the child to the extent the estate has been created by Husband or Husband's family;

____ the duty of care, control, protection, and reasonable discipline of the child;

____ the duty to support the child, including providing the child with clothing, food, shelter, and medical and dental care not involving an invasive procedure;

____ the right to consent for the child to medical and dental care not involving an invasive procedure;

____ the right to direct the moral and religious training of the child;

____ the right to consent to medical, dental, and surgical treatment involving invasive procedures;

____ the right to consent to psychiatric and psychological treatment;

____ the right to receive and give receipt for periodic payments for the support of the child and to hold or disburse these funds for the benefit of the child;

____ the right to represent the child in legal action and to make other decisions of substantial legal significance concerning the child;

____ the right to consent to the child's marriage, enlistment in the armed forces of the United States;

____ the right to make decisions concerning the child's education;

____ the right to the services and earnings of the child;

____ except when a guardian of the child's estate or a guardian or attorney ad litem has been appointed for the child, the right to act as agent of the child in relation to the child's estate if the child's action is required by a state, the United States, or a foreign government.

Wife shall have the rights and duties checked below:

____ the right to receive information from any other conservator of the child concerning the health education, and welfare of the child;

____ the right to confer with the other parent to the extent possible before making a decision concerning the health education and welfare of the child;

____ the right of access to medical, dental, psychological, and educational records of the child;

____ the right to consult with a physician, dentist, or psychologist of the child;

____ the right to consult with school officials concerning the child's welfare and educational status, including school activities;

____ the right to attend school activities;

____ the right to be designated on the child's records as a person to be notified in case of an emergency;

____ the right to consent to medical, dental, and surgical treatment during an emergency involving an immediate danger to the health and safety of the child;

____ the right to manage the estate of the child to the extent the estate has been created by Wife and or Wife's family.

____ the duty of care, control, protection, and reasonable discipline of the child;

____ the duty to support the child, including providing the child with clothing, food, shelter, and medical and dental care not involving an invasive procedure;

____ the right to consent for the child to medical and dental care not involving an invasive procedure;

____ the right to direct the moral and religious training of the child;

____ the right to consent to medical, dental, and surgical treatment involving invasive procedures;

____ the right to consent to psychiatric and psychological treatment;

____ the right to receive and give receipt for periodic payments for the support of the child and to hold or disburse these funds for the benefit of the child;

____ the right to represent the child in legal action and to make other decisions of substantial legal significance concerning the child;

____ the right to consent to the child's marriage, enlistment in the armed forces of the United States;

____ the right to make decisions concerning the child's education;

____ the right to the services and earnings of the child;

____ except when a guardian of the child's estate or a guardian or attorney ad litem has been appointed for the child, the right to act as agent of the child in relation to the child's estate if the child's action is required by a state, the United States, or a foreign government;

Visitation

Father shall have possession of the child(ren), as set forth below:

____ at any and all times mutually agreed to in advance by the parties and, failing mutual agreement, shall have possession of the child(ren) under the specified terms set out in the Standard Possession Order as set forth by Chapter 153, Subchapter F, of the Texas Family Code, which is incorporated herein and made a part hereof for all purposes including the following elections or deviations:

_____

_____

_____

_____

_____

____ in accordance with the schedule attached hereto as Exhibit "A" and made a part hereof for all purposes.

____ at all times mutually agreed upon between the child(ren) and Father.

____ at all times except for those periods specifically allocated to Mother as set forth herein.

Mother shall have possession of the child(ren), as set forth below:

____ at any and all times mutually agreed to in advance by the parties and, failing mutual agreement, shall have possession of the child(ren) under the specified terms set out in the Standard Possession Order as set forth by Chapter 153, Subchapter F, of the Texas Family Code, which is incorporated herein and made a part hereof for all purposes including the following elections or deviations:

_____

_____

_____

_____

_____

____ in accordance with the schedule attached hereto as Exhibit "A" and made a part hereof for all purposes.

____ at all times mutually agreed upon between the child(ren) and Mother.

____ at all times except for those periods specifically allocated to Father as set forth herein.

The child(ren) will be exchanged as set forth below:

_____ shall pick up the child(ren) from the residence of _____ at the beginning of each period of possession awarded to _____ and _____ shall return the child(ren) to _____ at the residence of _____ at the conclusion of each period of possession.

_____ shall pick up the child(ren) from their school or daycare or the residence of _____, whichever location is appropriate, at the beginning of each period of possession of awarded to _____ and _____ shall return the child(ren) to _____ their school or daycare or the residence of _____, whichever location is appropriate, at the conclusion of each period of possession.

_____ All pickups or delivery of the children shall take place at _____

_____

_____

Child Support

_____ shall pay child support to _____ in the amount of $_____ per [week] [month], with the first payment being due and payable on the first pay period following the date of the entry of the decree, and a like payment being due and payable on the same day of each [week] [month] thereafter until the date of the earliest occurrence of one of the following events:

(1) the child reaches the age of 18 years, provided that, if the child is fully enrolled in an accredited primary or secondary school in a program leading toward a high school diploma, the periodic child-support payments shall continue to be due and paid until the end of the school year in which the child graduates;

(2) the child marries;

(3) the child dies;

(4) the child's disabilities are otherwise removed for general purposes;

(5) the child is otherwise emancipated; or

(6) further order of the Court.

The following additional agreements shall be applicable:

____ (If more than one child) thereafter child support shall be $_____ per [week] [month] thereafter until the next date of the earliest occurrence of one of the events set forth above.

A wage garnishment order shall be entered for the payment of child support.

____ The wage withholding order will not be served on the employer of payor until such time as payor is in default on the payment of monthly child support.

_____shall provide and pay for health insurance for the child(ren).

All health care expenses not paid by insurance and incurred by or on behalf of the parties' child (ren), including, without limitation, the yearly deductible and medical, prescription drug, psychiatric, psychological, dental, eye care, ophthalmological, and orthodontic charges shall be paid:

_____ fifty (50%) percent by each parent

_____ or ____% by Husband and ____% by Wife

_____ shall maintain life insurance coverage in the amount of $_____ on his/her life with _____ as irrevocable beneficiary in trust for the child(ren) so long as he or she is obligated to pay child support for the child(ren). _____ shall provide proof of insurance once each calendar year to _____ upon request.

The child support provisions of this agreement shall be an obligation of the estate of _____ and shall not terminate on the death of _____. Payments received for the benefit of the child(ren) through life insurance, from the Social Security Administration or Department of Veterans Affairs or other governmental agency shall be a credit against this obligation.

Spousal Support

_____ shall pay spousal maintenance to _____ in the amount of $_____ per [week] [month], with the first payment being due and payable on the first pay period following the date of the entry of the decree, and a like payment being due and payable on the same day of each [week] [month] thereafter until _____ .
Spousal maintenance shall terminate upon the first to occur of the following checked events:

_____ death of payor.

_____ death of recipient.

_____ remarriage of recipient.

_____ payment of_____.

_____ _____.

Property

Husband, shall be awarded all right, title and interest in and to the property set forth below:

All clothing, jewelry, and other personal effects in Husband's possession, unless express provision is made herein to the contrary.

All household furniture, furnishings, fixtures, goods, appliances, and equipment in Husband's possession, unless express provision is made herein to the contrary.

The following items of personal property in the possession or control of Wife, which shall be made available to Husband by Wife to pick up on _____ between the hours of _____:

_____

_____

_____

_____

_____

_____

Any and all sums, whether matured or unmatured, accrued or unaccrued, vested or otherwise, together with all increases thereof, the proceeds there from, and any other rights related to any profit-sharing plan, retirement plan, pension plan, or like benefit program, such as social security, existing by reason of Husband's past, present, or future employment save and except those specific sums or interest awarded herein to Wife.

Any and all sums of cash in Husband's possession or subject to his sole control, including money on account in banks, savings institutions, or other financial institutions, which accounts stand in his sole name or from which he has the sole right to withdraw funds or which are subject to his sole control and/or the following specific accounts:

_____

_____

_____

_____

_____

_____

An interest in Wife's retirement income/benefits as follows:

_____

_____

_____

_____

A Qualified Domestic Relations Order shall be entered to effect this disposition as may be required or allowed by each plan.

An interest in Wife's employment related accounts and plans including but not limited to deferred compensation plans, savings plans and stock plans and stock option plans as follows:

_____

_____

_____

_____

_____

_____

A Qualified Domestic Relations Order shall be entered to effect this disposition as may be required or allowed by each plan.

Any and all stocks, bonds, and securities, registered in Husband's name, together with all dividends, splits, and other rights and privileges in connection therewith.

The real property, including but not limited to any escrow funds, prepaid insurance, utility deposits, keys, house plans, warranties and service contracts, and title and closing documents, described commonly as:

_____

_____

_____

Any and all policies of life insurance (including cash values) insuring Husband's life.

The following motor vehicle(s) together with all applicable insurance, warranties, title documents and keys:

_____

_____

_____

$_____ cash payable to Husband by Wife on or before _____, by cash, cashier's check, or money order.

The following business interests or other assets:

_____

_____

_____

_____

_____

_____

All frequent flyer miles in Husband's name.

Wife shall be awarded all rights, title, and interest in and to the property set forth below:

All clothing, jewelry, and other personal effects in Wife's possession, unless express provision is made herein to the contrary.

All household furniture, furnishings, fixtures, goods, appliances, and equipment in Wife's possession, unless express provision is made herein to the contrary.

The following items of personal property in the possession or control of Husband shall be made available to Wife by Husband to pick up on _____ between the hours of _____:

Any and all sums, whether matured or unmatured, accrued or unaccrued, vested or otherwise, together with all increases thereof, the proceeds therefrom, and any other rights related to any profit-sharing plan, retirement plan, pension plan, or like benefit program, such as social security, existing by reason of Wife's past, present, or future employment save and except those specific sums or interest awarded herein to Husband.

Any and all sums of cash in Wife's possession or subject to her sole control, including money on account in banks, savings institutions, or other financial institutions, which accounts stand in her sole name or from which she has the sole right to withdraw funds or which are subject to her sole control and/or the following specific accounts:

An interest in Husband's retirement income/benefits as follows:

A Qualified Domestic Relations Order shall be entered to effect this disposition as may be required or allowed by each plan.

An interest in Husband's employment-related accounts and plans including but not limited to deferred compensation plans, savings plans and stock plans and stock option plans as follows:

_____

_____

_____

_____

A Qualified Domestic Relations Order shall be entered to effect this disposition as may be required or allowed by each plan.

Any and all stocks, bonds, and securities, registered in Wife's name, together with all dividends, splits, and other rights and privileges in connection therewith.

The real property, including but not limited to any escrow funds, prepaid insurance, utility deposits, keys, house plans, warranties and service contracts, and title and closing documents, described commonly as:

_____

_____

Any and all policies of life insurance (including cash values) insuring Wife's life.

The following motor vehicle(s):

_____

_____

_____

$_____ cash payable to Wife by Husband on or before _____, by cash, cashier's check, or money order.

The following business interests or other assets:

_____

_____

_____

_____

_____

_____

All frequent flyer miles in Wife's name.

Sale of Real Property

The parties agree that the real property and all improvements located thereon commonly referred to as: _____ be sold under the terms and conditions and conditions checked below:

_____ The parties may attempt to sell the property without it being listed with a duly licensed real estate broker.

_____ The parties may list the property with a duly licensed real estate broker having sales experience in the area where the property is located.

_____ The parties shall list the property with a duly licensed real estate broker having sales experience in the area where the property is located, provided further that such real estate broker shall be an active member in the Multiple Listing Service with the _____ Board of Realtors.

_____ The property shall be sold for a price that is mutually agreeable to Husband and Wife. Should Husband and Wife be unable to agree on a sales price, upon the application of either party to this suit, the property shall be sold under such terms and conditions as determined by a court-appointed receiver.

_____ [Husband] [Wife] shall continue to make all payments of principal, interest, taxes, and insurance on the property during the pendency of the sale, and [Husband] [Wife] shall have the exclusive right to enjoy the use and possession of the premises until closing. All maintenance and repairs necessary to keep the property in its present condition shall be paid by [Husband] [Wife] or as follows:

_____

_____

_____

_____

_____

_____

_____ The net sales proceeds (which are defined as the gross sales price less costs of sale and full payment of any mortgage indebtedness or liens on the property) are hereby distributed as follows:

_____

_____

_____

_____

_____

As part of the division of the estate of the parties, Husband, shall pay, and indemnify and hold Wife harmless from, the following debts and obligations:

the balance due and owing for liabilities secured by property awarded to Husband herein;

any and all debts incurred by Husband from and after the date of the parties' separation on or about _____ .

the following specific debts:

_____

_____

_____

_____

_____

_____

_____

_____

As part of the division of the estate of the parties, Wife, shall pay, and indemnify and hold Husband harmless from, the following debts and obligations:

the balance due and owing for liabilities secured by property awarded to Wife herein;

any and all debts incurred by Wife from and after the date of the parties' separation on or about _____ .

the following specific debts:

_____

_____

_____

_____

_____

Attorney's fees and costs incurred by Husband shall be paid by Husband except as follows:

_____

_____

Attorney's fees and costs incurred by Wife shall be paid by Wife except as follows:

_____

_____

Federal Income Taxes

The parties shall be liable for federal incomes taxes follows:

Jointly liable for all taxes due from the date of marriage through _____.

Husband shall be responsible for and shall pay and hold wife harmless from all taxes due for the period of_____.

Wife shall be responsible for and shall pay and hold Husband harmless from all taxes due for the period of_____.

The parties shall share federal income tax refunds as follows:

Equally for the years _____

Husband shall be entitled to the entire refund for the years

_____.

Wife shall be entitled to the entire refund for the years

_____.

Specific deductions:

Husband shall be allowed to claim the following deductions on his separate return:

Deduction	Year
_____	_____
_____	_____
_____	_____

Wife shall be allowed to claim the following deductions on her separate return:

Deduction	Year
_____	_____
_____	_____
_____	_____

Federal income tax child dependency exemptions are awarded as follows:

Wife is awarded the exemption for the following children _____ for _ and all subsequent (odd/even) years.

Husband is awarded the exemption for the following children

_____

for _____ and all subsequent (odd/even) years.

The parties agree to execute all instruments necessary to effect this mediation settlement including but not limited to the following documents:

Final Decree of Divorce (To be prepared by_____)

Employers Withholding Order (To be prepared by _____)

Special Warranty Deed (To be prepared by _____)

Deed of Trust To Secure Assumption (To be prepared by _____)

Power of Attorneys (___) (To be prepared by _____)

QDROs (___) (Wife's plan(s) (To be prepared by _____)

QDROs (___) (Husband's plan(s) (To be prepared by _____)

Mediation

The parties agree to mediation with Roy Ghassemi Mediation services prior to instituting any modification proceedings except for a true emergency involving the health, safety, or welfare of the child.

This agreement is made and performable in the county of suit, and shall be construed in accordance with the laws of the State of Texas and commenced upon the date of signing herein.

Each signatory to this settlement agreement has entered into the same freely and voluntarily and without duress after having consulted with legal or other professionals or after having been given an opportunity to consult with legal or other professionals elected not to do so.

AGREED TO THIS ___ DAY OF _____, 20___.

_____   _____

ASG, Wife   HWG, Husband

Signed in accordance with Sec. 6.602 (b) (3) and Sec. 153.0071(d) (3), Texas Family Code:

_____   _____

Attorney for Wife   Attorney for Husband

WITNESSED:

_____

Roy Ghassemi PhD.
Mediator
EXHIBIT _____

CHAPTER 10

Changes After the Divorce Is Final Just Like Any Traditional Divorce

You may always change the terms and conditions that have been set in your divorce settlement. Therefore, if you know your circumstances may change or you think your life plans and your future may change in any form or shape, you always have the option of having the settlement modified or changed.

"Once an agreement is signed, it can only be changed by agreement of both parties. Once it becomes part of your divorce judgment, it can only be changed by another court order (which could be based on an agreement you come to)" (Bryan Driscoll, "What Is A Divorce Settlement Agreement? (2023 Guide)," *Forbes*, July 26, 2022, forbes. com/advisor/legal/divorce/divorce-settlement-agreement).

In a traditional divorce, you have to have an attorney redraw and modify the settlement of your divorce, and then he would have to contact the other attorney to present the modification to him, and he would have to contact their client and review the new modification to have it changed and get you to accept it. Of course, with this option, you are starting a new process that would involve an extra amount of time and money, which can be prevented by using mediation.

But with mediation, all you have to do is to contact the original mediator or another mediator and meet with him together and have them redraw the final settlement. If there is a need for renegotiation, you can do it right there and then without having to spend the extra time and money to use the attorneys.

In many divorces, the fact of knowing that by using the attorneys to renegotiate for you, you have to go through the whole process and the agony you have experienced when you got divorced. That makes many people change their minds and not even ask for what they wanted to modify in their settlement. Everybody's life changes after divorce, especially when there are children involved. Therefore, it is natural that one would see the need to have changes in the divorce, so it is better to know you can have this option and receive what you really want instead of just dealing with what you have settled with when the circumstances were different when you got separated.

Furthermore, as long as both sides agree on their separation agreement to have a clause for future discussing in case any future issue or problem that rises which would encourage both parties to have a better understanding and relationship to contact the mediators when that time comes.

At that time, the mediator will set a time for both sides to schedule a mediation session, and in that session, the mediator will help renegotiate that or those issues in question and get both sides to agree on them. At that time the mediator would write a rider as an attachment that would be incorporated and executed to be attached to the original agreement.

NOTES

-
-
-
-
-
-
-
-
-
-
-
-
-
-
-
-
-
-

NOTES

-
-
-
-
-
-
-
-
-
-
-
-
-
-
-
-
-
-

INDEX

www.ingramcontent.com/pod-product-compliance
Lightning Source LLC
Chambersburg PA
CBHW021451210526
45463CB00002B/728